Bird of Paradise

Selected Poems, 1968-2011

Hugh David Loxdale

BRAMBLEBY BOOKS

Bird of Paradise: Selected Poems 1968-2011
Copyright©Hugh David Loxdale 2011

ISBN 9781908241016

Published 2011 by
Brambleby Books Ltd., UK
www.brambleby.books.co.uk

Cover painting by Laura Swale
Cover design by Tanya Warren, Creatix
Printed by Good News Digital Books, UK

Bird of Paradise

To Nischi, with all my love

About the Book

This collection of 84 poems explores, amongst other things, the variety and diversity of the natural world, from earthworms and insects to humans, to the English countryside, to dramatic waterfalls, to the vagaries of the weather, in all its glory, viewed with the author's wry philosophical perspective.

About the Author

Hugh David Loxdale was born in Horley, Surrey, England, but grew up in Hemel Hempstead, Hertfordshire, where he spent much of his spare time outside school roaming the countryside and observing wildlife. Besides an interest in science, especially biology, he is also interested in history and English literature. He started writing poetry in his late teens, although eventually decided to embark on a career in entomology rather than literature. After gaining degrees in Zoology at Reading and Oxford Universities, he published his first collection of predominantly natural history poetry, *The Eternal Quest*, in 1988 (Merlin Books Ltd., Braunton, Devon) under the pseudonym of 'Hugh Llewelyn', one branch of his maternal ancestors having come from Wales. His next collection of 84 poems, *Blue Skies in Tuscany*, was published in 2000 by Minerva Press, London, and again concerned mainly natural history themes, but with a distinct philosophical slant. Thereafter, he published a further seven collections of poetry with Brambleby Books. The present volume is his eighth, also with a natural history bias. He is married and presently lives with his wife Nicola in Jena, Germany, where he works as a professional entomologist.

Preface

This selection of my poetry was written at various times and in various places, but mainly at Batford, near Harpenden, Hertfordshire, during the period 1993-2006 (poems no. 1, 2, 4, 5, 8-15, 17-37, 39, 41-43, 45-60, 64, 66, 71, 73, 76-80), and Jena, Germany, (poems no. 50, 59, 67, 81-84) from 2006-11. The poem *Fifty Years on* (65) was one of the first poems I ever wrote and was composed whilst I was still at Apsley Grammar School (now Longdean School), Hemel Hempstead, Hertfordshire, in 1968. The remaining poems were written as follows: *Foggy Moon* (6) and *Human Resources* (7) on Nevis, West Indies, in 2000; *Ambition* (44) and *City of Flitwick* (63) in Flitwick, Bedfordshire, in 1987 and 1989, respectively; *Books* (3) at Reading University, Berkshire, in 2001; *I have known* (16) at Mount Vernon Hospital, Middlesex, in 2001; *Where the Iguassu falls* (40) whilst I stayed near the falls to attend an international entomological congress held in Brazil in 2000; *The Goat* (38) at Faugeré, Deux-Sèvres, France, in 1995; the poem *Clouded Yellow* (61) at Pylos, Greece, in 2002; *On Kings, Cola and Zola* (74) in Augsburg, Germany, in 2003; *August Moon* (62) at Utting, Germany, in 2002; *Foreign Dogs* (68) and *Beauty* (75) in South Kensington, London, in 2004 and 2006, respectively; *Kookaburra's Laugh* (69) in Brisbane, Australia, in 2004, whilst I attended another international entomological congress; *A Day Spent at Tenby* (70) at Tenby, south Wales, in 2006; and the *Last Day of 2005* (72) in Edinburgh, Scotland, in 2005.

Hugh D. Loxdale
Jena, Germany, 6th March, 2011

Contents

Bird of Paradise

You are my bird of paradise,
The girl of my tropical dreams,
Near turquoise seas and hibiscus flowers
And foliage that glints and gleams.

You are my bird of paradise,
A goddess fallen to earth,
By coral sands and waving palms,
Like the sun kissing the surf.

You are my bird of paradise,
A creature of shapely form,
With an enchanting smile and shining eyes,
And a heart most kind and warm.

You are my bird of paradise,
A species of exotic being,
Below volcanic cones and forest streams
Where believing is indeed seeing.

You are that bird of paradise,
Who I will love to my dying day,
Come monsoons and wild hurricanes…
Till my last breath is cast away.

Bats in Batford

There are not many bats in Batford,
Few that I have seen,
On soft summer evenings
When the Moon is apple green.

Although the Pipistrelle visits from time to time
Our little garden and smaller pond,
To flit across dark waters
Of which the amphibians are so fond.

Whilst ghost swift moths
With silvery wings, play amongst the grass,
Spectres of the sunless hours
That endless seem to pass.

And further beyond, in Sauncey Wood,
Where anemones in May white bloom,
The long-eared owls, with studied gaze,
Hoot and sporadic boom.

Or watch in silence the forest floor
Amidst the tree-lined halls
For signs of life within the leaves,
The wood mice and common voles.

But there is alas no belfry here,
Even so, bluebells still chime
Where the chaffinch sings his cheerful song
As the Sun awakes sublime.

Books

Books, various and colourful,
Adorn the naked shelf,
Rather as clothes, the naked self.

Reflections of the inner man...

His (or her) loves, desires, fears, obsessions...

All positive qualities, they surround him,
Show him who he really is,
Or at least, to what he may aspire
And indeed, what he is not.

They leave him little room for doubt,
These books, who may amuse, beguile, frighten
And even chide him.

They are, after all, his friends,
And when they are lent or are gone missing –
By fair means or foul –
Their absence cries out...

Not like a missing tooth in an aged jaw,
More the absence of familiarity
Of a well-respected and beloved friend
Somehow gone away.

He is jealous for their safe return.

No electronic wizardry,
Bites or RAMs,
Can substitute for these boon companions,
Kind soul mates of the lonely, reflective hours.

Ultimately, just to see them sitting there
In their loyal ranks is comfort enough,
Let alone read them all over again.

As for other people's books,
Why even their titles
Can be enough to give him indigestion,
Whilst ignoring the strange (and sometimes distasteful)
Substance between their covers,
Never perused,
As bigotry can testify.

Earthworm

There is was, on the road...
Washed out of its home, its burrow,
Its place of refuge, by the heavy rain
Storms of last night, fourteen centimetres long
Or thereabouts, pink, naked and vulnerable,
Squirming, yet even so determined as it
Elongated its narrow head and retracted its tail
(both indistinguishable from one another) and
Made rapidly – and blindly – towards the nearby
Playing fields (or were they killing fields?), easy
Victim to the roving eye of blackbird and thrush, or
The teeth of the lawn mower, so desirous to reduce
Everything in its path to a verdant swayd, almost a
Green desert.

I too had to move on quickly, so could not observe
Its plight further – whether it was squashed by some
Approaching vehicle or made it to the relative safety
Of the grass beyond. However, what I did notice in
Those few seconds, was that it was not wholly pink.
Instead, it was a shade of brick red at the front,
Through to light grey, with a nut brown 'saddle'
And continuing on to a sandy yellow tail
– a spectrum of colours in fact.

As the worm turned, I left it there –
Slimy but rather beautiful,
And, as with so much beauty,
Apparently very
Fragile.

Blossom in May

This was an era of blossom,
The hours of its greatest delight,
Cherry, blackthorn and mespil,
Delicate, pink and white.

And magnolia, large and lovely,
Its petals carpeting the floor,
Marking the high-tide of springtime,
The wettest that any man saw.

So that he gave a cursory glance skyward,
As the clouds gathered to glower,
And cut dead the bright sunshine
To provoke another shower.

But all that fell at that glad time
To blow and dust the street,
Were those tiny little fragments
Torn from a much larger sheet.

Snow they did, for many days,
Whilst the tulips gathered strength,
And the daffodils relinquished their potent spell,
One that had charmed at length...

When sparrows chirp and Six Bells ring,
Along St. Michael's† narrow way,
The Sun regains its power to warm
On this most glorious fifth of May.

† St. Michael's Street, St. Albans, Hertfordshire, U.K.

Foggy Moon

Oh Foggy Moon, Oh Foggy Moon,
I saw you yesterday,
High up in the pale blue sky –
A sharp crescent holding sway.

Today you appear absent,
Missing from your post;
I looked for you everywhere
Inland and towards the coast.

Only a few days ago
You were full and golden round,
As clear as a bell you were,
Although made not a single sound.

At other times you were hazy,
Enveloped in veils of mist,
Your poetry and mystery,
Hard for any to resist.

I have also seen you peeping
From behind a silver cloud,
Too shy to reveal your presence,
Or too infernally proud.

Oh Foggy Moon, Oh Foggy Moon,
Please do come back again,
And show yourself to your admirers,
In the sunshine, night or rain.

Human Resources

Does this term refer to us,
Men and women born ever free?
Or to base-born slaves
Held in captivity?

Whose lives are not their own,
Treated like cattle kept,
Who must obey their master's voice,
Answered in perennial debt.

A destiny robbed and taken,
Their free will denied them too,
With chains to hold and bind them,
And prove their reality true.

To make them work in the hot Sun,
Or crush the sullen cane,
In mills high up on the hillsides,
Subjected to lashing rain.

Or worse still, some ghastly resource,
Dreamt up by an inhuman mind,
Whose very bodies, not just their souls,
Are used by a perverse mankind.

Have we then learnt nothing
Over these sad and turbulent years?
Surely life's not worth living
Without freedom...ringing in our ears.

So let us thus go forward
Into uplands both sunny and free,
And abolish such obnoxious terms,
And defend our liberty.

Clockwork Orange

Every day,
As regular as clockwork,
Joe[†] consumes an orange
Or two, usually…
Our dear statistical friend,
His head full of facts,
Acts out the ritual
Of slowly and deliberately
Peeling the fruit,
Shiny and spherical…
After the main course…

As well as rooting
Out the sensitivities
Of his near neighbours,
Their loves and hates,
Their bold and unruly
Pretensions…

He bends their ears,
But rarely elicits tears
At the lunch table…
Where only the strong
Survive,
Indeed thrive
Amidst the sounds of war,
The smell of acrid juice
And the cries of the righteous,
Now highly wound up…
Or the piteous whimpers
Of the vanquished…

It is certainly
All most strange…
And striking,
Especially that we regularly
Come back…
For more.

† Professor Joseph N. Perry, D.Sc., formerly senior
  statistician at Rothamsted Research, Harpenden,
  Herts., U.K.

Freedom

I may be fifty...
But then again at least I am free...
Now that I have left
The steel carapace
On its wheels behind...
To traverse the environment.
To smell, for myself,
Spring in the air.
To see the snowdrops shaking, in fits,
In the unforgiving February wind;
To hear the chaffinch delight its friends
In song...and me...
At the height of a lime tree,
Sentinel to the avenue beyond;
Watch the redwings pass quickly
From branch to branch
And glimpse the ruddy plumage once
At a wing's base.

I feel sorry for the young.
Trapped in bucket seats behind tinted glass.
Whisked from pillar to post,
Almost free, but in fact not quite.
Deprived of sunlight, of vitamins,
Of the chance to fight,
They stare out, odd pale fish
From behind their luxurious tanks.
Weak bones denied the possibility
Of strength and endurance;
Their muscles and sinews too.

Where will they be in two score years hence –
Saved from bullies and the cruel wind's wrath?
Striding strongly into the future
Along woodland paths strewn with wild flowers?

23

Or more like limp jellyfish,
Stranded on some lonely beach
To glisten and wobble
In the receding tide…and Sun,
Slaves of their parent's concern
And wealth…
That has left them unfit
Hardly to face another Spring?

Easter Evening

On closing the glass doors
Against the natural world,
Shutting out the wind
And never ending rain
That has fallen continuously,
Or so it seems,
All this prolonged era
At the Millennium's turn.

Cocooning myself into the
Warmth and selfish comfort within,
Barrier from the cruel elements
And the primitive, unrestrained forces
Without...

I pause for a moment,
As the already dark evening sky
Gets even darker.

The sound of rain is incessant...
Drowning out all other senses,
Imagined or real, prophesised or happened...

I once catch the voice
Of the blackbird's thrall.

Happy, near, round words
Of joy.

Words from a black creature
Too black now to see,
Even silhouetted in the despondent space
Beyond the still naked ash tree.

I hear him calling.
I receive his message loud and clear.
Layer upon layer of melody,
Enwrapped, chord upon chord
To frame a beauteous tune...
Far beyond our mortal understanding
And the wisdom of our untutored ears.

A song – like Christ's love,
To enrich all millennia,
Not just this over-sold, plastic one,
The here and now...
But a song that spreads its blessing
Far and wide...

On outstretched wings
Reaching backwards in time
And onwards... to that
Age-old prospect
Of the expectant – the future...

Uniting and embracing each and all
With his glory.

Five o'clock

Five o'clock, the clock says so,
The starling relates all joy...
On this most perfect
Of May days.

The zephyr sighs; the water falls,
Tumbling and babbling nearby.

Only the bumblebees apparently know
That even, as the daylight hours subside,
There is yet so much to do.

The pond is cleared; the frogs return;
The neighbours dig their land.

Clouds roll in from the east
To cancel out the blue.

A dog barks; rooks take wing;
The low, silent swifts speak rain.

A transience belies the pressing calm...

And soon, as must, the time is ripe
When I must also go.

The Waitress

The waitress
From the Norfolk Arms[†]
In the small black dress,
With dark stockings
And shapely legs,
Uses her charms –
Of which she is fully aware –
Her sexuality
Like a flail
As she flows
About her business,
Tray in hand,
Without a care,
Serving the customers,
Mostly male,
Her vivacity
And infectious laugh
Enough to evoke
Admiration…and a flush
From the crustiest
Bachelor…and sometimes gay,
Who beat a path
To this place…
Her brunette, cropped hair,
Button nose
And delicate white hands
Giving pleasure
Every day,
Amongst the regulars, rarely plush,
Who sip their beer
And chew their food,
And talk amongst themselves,
Their eyes held
Distractedly, yet firmly fixed,
On this belle
Of the London scene,

A queen amongst queens.
And though no beauty as such
In the formal sense, emits
That fragrance
Of personality,
That pungent animal force
That pervades
All…it seems,
Down to their very socks…
And into their dreams.

† South Kensington, London

The Health Industry

The hospital is like an industry.

The raw material comes in at one end –
The patients.

They are duly seen, diagnosed, treated.

Most survive, some do not.

Is this just life 'writ large'?

That we are interfering with
The blind watch maker's watch.
His most glorious and divine creation?

Trying to make it tick faster,
Or better…or at all.

Redwood Trees

Redwood trees rear up very erect
Towards the sky, seeking out
The clouds and the bright stars beyond.
They are lofty plants indeed.

I look up into the green crown from far below,
Minimised by their huge presence,
Staring into the complex canopy of branches
And dark foliage.

Sometimes they drop their cones,
Small wooden spheres packed with tiny seeds
(a contrast between what is and is to become)
From on high, to resound with a thud
On the mat of dry leaves at their base…
A concession to the demands of gravity
And their defiance of it for so long –
Millennia – and to future generations.

Why even they must reproduce, to replace their kind
Who Jurassic monsters must have seen,
Hardly changed since then.

In my adoration, my frustration
Of frailty, both in stature and longevity,
I punch the thick, soft, fibrous bark…as many
Have done these long, lost centuries,
A protection against the ravages of fire, not men.

It is not hurt, nor my fist for that matter.

Perhaps if the trees could think, were conscious, they would
Query why men – no doubt some women too –
Have done this to them down the ages.
But how could they know, let alone understand,
Our longings for immortality, for recognition.

They have it all, or as much as one can get to savour.
And they are unlikely to relinquish their perception
Of reality…and of truth.

Meanwhile, the Steller's Jay hops and calls
Mysteriously through
The thick branches, half out of sight,
Half mystery itself…
Leaving me alone to ponder the
Awesome perspective of time and
The preciousness of things…living.

Foot and Mouth

The spectator
Of that ghastly scene –
Burning the innocents –
Stands witness
Like a little child,
To avert its gaze,
Or cover its eyes with small hands,
Hoping against hope
That it is all in the mind.

That when it lets in the light anew...
Lambs will be dancing
In those meadows few,
Gambolling and greeting
Ever fresh, the happy
Force of Spring.

Cows will be un-phased
By the dead sounds
Of the cool marksman's aim
And its quick resolution.
Will graze on, survivors
All...

Whilst the curious pigs,
Always keen to grub about
And meet the challenge
Of a new dawn,
(That now lie slaughtered in lean ranks,
Shot without a trial),
May still snort and snuffle
Possessed of one sense,
Perhaps rooted in that
Gnarled, dark body,

The truffle,
Spark – and joy of priceless
Life…

More intelligent – and kind
Than is presently in our power,
A gift of madness.

I have known

I have known cold courage,
Have seen that bold sangfroid,
The triumph of great dignity,
Here on the cancer ward.

The patients with their ashen face,
Their bodies cruelly sick
Endure the fearful enemy
And the catheter's hurtful nick.

They stand and sit with book in hand,
Testament to their will to fight,
The assailant of the hidden soul
That seeks to impose its might.

But it can never, ever win,
Whilst such brave hearts do beat,
Who desperately storm the barricades...
And never once retreat.

It Is So Sad

It is so sad,
And I wonder why,
That they are so reticent,
And so shy
Who look at their feet
And not the sky,
When they come into work...
As if to die?

Is it Society
Or their genes
That has so cowered,
Or so it seems?

Maybe it's one, the other
Or both,
That crushes spontaneity,
And squanders growth?

Language

Language is like a bird.

However, it is no stuffed specimen in a glass case,
staring out into the rude world with beady, brown,
disconsolate eyes. Nor rarely that endangered, hardly
extant, species in a gilded cage, waiting patiently
for the day when the door may, by chance, be left wide open
to allow it to escape...and find a soul-mate.

More, it is that truly wild spirit that needs
the freedom of the rustling air...and perishes without.
It maintains a desire to preen; to keep its beautiful
feathers continuously in shape; to exercise its pectoral
muscles...and thereby strengthen them...so that one day,
each day, it may launch itself into that glistening place
of colours and shapes, shades and images; of forest, plain,
marsh, mountain and the city streets.

To fly up high, so high, circle around, dive, wheel, bank, loop,
veer, yaw, roll in the blueness of the sun-drenched heavens...
and then safely land...back to earth...

Confident that it has achieved the impossible;
defied gravity; done what those around perhaps
thought could not be done. Proved to itself and all the world...that
it has left the nest, and is here to stay,
and that nothing...can ever be the same again. It has arrived.
Found and engaged others of its vibrant kind.
Lasted the test of time...and space.
Communicated its presence and its passions,
and gained the living, ethereal power...of existence.

Dog Woman of Rothamsted Park

The slim woman
With her two black dogs –
Labradors both –
Strides up the lime avenue
Between the trees,
Virtually bare of leaves,
Crossing each shadow's bar,
Marching determinedly onward
In her bright red cap, blue cagoule
And faded jeans.
Ever forward, the low winter
Sun at her left ...
Whilst the dogs,
Their eyes never far from her,
Sniff and wag, run to visit each
Spot of interest,
Follow their mistress,
The leader of the pack
With confidence, purpose,
Determination...
Even as she begins
To become smaller
In the scheme of perspective...
They mark her well
Out of the corner
Of their gleaming eyes,
Haunt her, follow her
Relentlessly
Almost a magnetic bond
Exists...to bind them.

Only as she rounds
The hill
Do they catch her up,

Panting, belching steam,
Wet, shaggy, doggy,
Tails up, lips and eyes in a smile,
They come to heel,
To feel the warmth
Of her touch
As she gains control,
Re-asserts her authority,
Puts the true reins on
To lead them to a promised land…
And then home.

Just before hand,
Out of nowhere,
Two Springer Spaniels engage,
They are attracted and attractive,
But as they close
Have second thoughts
Of an encounter.

Like silly bitches
They gamble and spoil
The dewy grass,
Their long, thick fur flowing,
Turning, dancing, tumbling
Over each other,
Biting in mock attack.
They swirl, around and around
Their owners until…
Collapsing in a tortuous pile.
They fade…
Hot dogs indeed.

Until then,
I had never seen
What was the attraction of dogs –
Smelly, slobbery, demanding,
Fawning…

That my thoughts had now changed;
That I could never again
Voice such views,
Be quite so full against
These favoured hounds,
Was as surprising to me then
As the sight of those happy, happy
Dogs, at play,
Seen unexpectedly…and with joy
On that cool winter's day.

Beloved Cat

Our beloved cat has passed away,
Never to be seen again,
No more her face at the window
In the sunshine or chilliest rain.

Never her stare from the shed roof top,
Her lying in front of the fire,
Never her waiting by the bathroom,
Or her trips into the garden, her desire.

She lived near on twelve years,
Apparently good for her kind.
I just pray she is now in heaven,
At peace in her body and mind.

She was indeed irreplaceable,
A character with lots of fun,
An example of just how precious life is…
Before its unique course is run.

The Last Mouse

She (our cat) has died today,
Victim of a malevolent gene.

Oh glad, happy being,
Comfort of our resting hours.
Why, did you not promise us
To be well, to live on...
Into this new golden age.
To battle against all the
Forces of wind, hail, snow and rain?

Claw your way forward
To that promised land
Where untold truths
Yet remain undiscovered?

Now your body lies in ruins.

We wish, so wish, it were not so.

But you were a fighter for life...
And a fearful hunter too.

Even as your lifeblood
Ebbed away,
Out you were,
Near your favourite hebe bush...
Where the lawn meets
The rickety garden fence...
To watch and wait
For your small companions,
The field mice,
Playmates to while away
The balmy hours of spring
When the daffodils,

Gorgeous in their yellow livery,
Nod and toss their heads,
Like racehorses,
Before the playful wind...
Whilst huge bumblebees ply their trade,
Despite the cutting air.

You were no friend to them (the mice) though...
And perhaps they knew it.

Why, you even brought one back
In your jaws,
Played with it on the uncut grass;
Tossed it around,
Stamped on its
With your satin paws
And then bit into its tiny, horror-struck
Head;
Savaged it until it
Were truly dead.

Your own fading mortality
Did not stop to make you think;
Change your attitude;
Alter your philosophy one iota...
To grant you that last great gift
Of compassion.

No, ultimately, your character won through.

The genes will have their say.

Your nature, the cruel nature of the hunter
Persevered up to the last hour, nay the last second
Of the last day...before judgement.

When Monika Was Here

When Monika was here we had some fun
Down in the sun-baked park[†],
Sitting under a shady tree
Watching the boys there lark...

Having come from the gloomy pub
Where we drank our beer ice-cold,
And recounted all our several lives
And what was yet foretold.

Though finally dived into a shop
With antiques from every land,
But only bought a brass butterfly
For our teapot on which to stand.

Not much, perhaps from all there was,
A plethora of wondrous riches,
Yet when we recount Monika's tales,
We are still reduced to stitches.

† Gadebridge Park, Hemel Hempstead, Hertfordshire.

Most of the Leaves have fallen

Most of the ash leaves have fallen,
Most of the birds flown away,
Now only the piebald magpie
Parades proud in its glistening array.

The mists hug close the green grass,
The cold air snubs the nose,
Hot breath teases the morning,
A pale sun weakly glows.

This year the acorns are absent,
They no longer litter the floor,
And Jack Frost may be young still,
But he's hard knocking at the door.

Dead Daffodils

Dead daffodils in a clear vase adorn,
Spring's promise, all forlorn,
Yet in the garden their sibs still thrive,
Proving the season is still much alive.

The Poppy
(Reflections on Armistice Day at the Millennium)

What does the poppy now signify
To those who love life, but yet may die
On battlefields and in bloody conflicts new,
Defending what is just and true?

Must we be vigilant, always strive
To keep liberty's hard-won flame alive,
So that in the future, ever more,
Is never seen that scourge of war?

That soldiers in that foreign field,
Fight to win and never yield;
All mother's sons and brothers too;
Bravest of the brave; fewest of the few.

Gone are the bombshells, the gun's crack,
Absent the bombers, and the flak;
Peace now straddles the healed lines,
In harmony and friendship, old age declines.

And the new order at the Millennium born,
To Europe's flag hope is sworn;
Young men may thus not die and women weep,
Whilst babes in gas masks unhappy sleep.

Though who recalls that great sacrifice,
Of those who fought and relinquished life;
Or those who survived the stolen years…
And held firm to stay our darkest fears?

With the turning of history's page,
Passes both misery and cold rage,
And with the setting of the unchanged sun,
Memories do recede, and fade, one by one.

Cupressus

Cupressus were not envisaged
As tools, the instruments to depress us:

Huge shapes watching over us,
Cutting out the Sun's magnificent rays,
Hemming us in,
They loom menacingly
At the very edge
Of many a garden plot.
Triffids in all but name.

Sucking the soil – and soul –
Of its goodness,
Its moisture too.

Restricting views, depriving neighbours
From themselves…and others…
Secluding, forcing isolation,
Demanding our veneration

They have their place sure…
In the land from whence they sprang…
To glory in landscapes
In their pillar form…

Though not in English suburbia…
Where their crushing, alien presence
Leads to many a depression,
Sad act of repression,
Relieved only by the tortured whine
Of the chain saw.

Perhaps then they deserve to be chopped –
Or put to flight –
And thereby, let in more light –
Literal and spiritual,
Just as God once said?

Epitaph for my Parents

The wind might blow,
The sunshine temporary fail,
But their courage never did
And their love remained true.

Me

I am myself, I am me,
I am not a King, Statesman, or a gnarled tree,
A soldier, sailor, nor airman too,
Although I have met such, years ago,
It is true.

Rather, I am a scientist, philosopher and perhaps wit,
Long hours at this desk, do I sit.

But most of all, I believe in you,
If only you could see this and if only you knew.

Ode to Miss Jackie Simpkins †

Goodbye Miss Simpkins,
Alas goodbye,
Your leaving here makes me sigh.

Your resolution and friendly style,
Your laughter, your cheery smile,

Your talk of cats…and politics too…
All so uncommon,
Discussed by few.

Your knowledge of bees,
And acceptance of fun…
A ray of sunshine?
No, a mini-Sun!

To gladden each worker's heart…and mind,
Be she (or he) a bee…
Or of humankind.

A rare gift, one so rare,
I'm sad you're going, it's so unfair.

† On leaving the Bee Department, Rothamsted Research,
  Harpenden, Hertfordshire.

Deadwood

The comment
is neither as old
nor as generous
as the baobab tree,
that sturdy relic
of the African plains
whose giant, bottle-shaped trunk,
full of water,
hides this from all
save the elephants
who tear at its flesh
until the rains
plunge from the terrifying skies,
and that which is dormant
cries out for life afresh
and springs to its release.
When the baobabs
the 'upside-down' tree,
with branches like roots,
yields milk-white flowers,
fruit and fingery leaves,
food for the bush baby and monkey alike,
an ancient being that deceives,
for nine months in twelve,
the animals,
save the elephants,
wiliest of them,
that it is dead.
Instead, it shelters securely
and gives that precious commodity.
So too, of human kind,
often written off as 'deadwood',
yet which should be revered,
the elderly ones, as wise
and parched as pachyderms,

sons and daughters of many a sage
who, as writers and musicians
might do
in their golden age,
give rise to their greatest glories –
plays, symphonies and many more,
'new shoots',
page after exquisite page.

Serengeti Society

All is well whilst you
Gallop with the herd
Across the vast, grass-ridden plains.

Kick your heels, wheel and dance,
Bite and bare your teeth,
Snort and snarl.

But woe betide you if you
Go out on a limb, or worse,
Break one…and start to limp,
Indeed, become limp.

Then, within hours,
Vultures swirl in ever-decreasing
Circles in the wide
Blue skies above.

The glowing eyes
Of jackal and hyena…
Faint at first,
Can be seen penetrating
The intangible gloom of dusk.

Whilst the coarse, reverberating
Roar of lions
From the nearby thicket is heard…
A death knell of sorts…
In the quietness of the evening air…
As the sun, red and beautiful,
Sinks once again below
The western horizon.

To be down is to be out.

And meanwhile, your comrades
Stare on, in some sort of horror,
Mixed with fascination.

Their eyes bulge, their tails swish,
Their brains try and take in all
That they are witnessing.

Yet still, they will do nothing.

After a while, they turn away,
Perhaps dejectedly,
To speed off into
The anonymity and collective
Comfort of night...
Mere shadows of their
Former selves.

Sonnet for my Love

How I love her beyond the bright rainbow,
This golden daughter of the Seasons' care,
She understands the logic of water,
The fragrant kisses of the summer air,
The tumbling mirth of the brown autumn leaves,
The coolness of the wintry sun's harsh eye.
She follows the ripples in the shallows,
The rugged flight of the white butterfly,
Drifting of the cloudlets at heaven's height,
Feckless in the largeness of the blue sky.
She dances in the sweet silken meadows,
Adrift with a myriad coloured blooms,
Sighs at the sad passing of the geese flocks,
And then weeps when the distant thunder booms.

Spring

Along the road,
By the ancient chestnut tree,
Much beloved of the
Children in the Fall,
The first chiff-chaff is heard
In this new Millennium;
A golden age?

Denotes the tide of spring,
Sweeping in
As it has always done,
Despite Man's
Arrangement of the years.

The brimstone male,
Seasoned survivor
Of the winter's gloom,
Rides now the warm zephyr's blast,
Casting away the drab
Residue of the coldness
And its damp retainer.

The small tortoiseshells,
and the peacock too,
Skit fast across the grass
And roof tops alike,
Mad with passion, –
They are unchained…
And free at last.

Then two bumblebees,
Huge queens from the underworld,
Visit the daffodils
Gladly…

Nodding sulphur heads
No less brilliant than the brimstone,
One of their number, escaped
Or so it seems…
To chase the swarming air.

But they are turned away
To fly in a circle,
Almost collide with me…
As I watch them go.

No not heralds of the season,
More its progenitors
The flesh that gives it being,
Whilst the sun is warm on the face.

I feel good.

I have survived…
To witness this miracle…

Anew.

The Sea

The sea, the sea, flows relentlessly;
It cannot be long stopped by gods and kings,
Let alone by you and me.

The sea, the sea, crashes endlessly,
Erases all traces of those sacred feet,
Oh so white, almost petite.

The sea, the sea, washes recklessly;
All land is fair game to its rapacious jaw,
Eroding cliffs from top to floor.

The sea, the sea, caresses sensuously,
Strokes gently the weathered rocks,
Waves swirling to soothe the dark brown locks.

The sea, the sea, life giver for all eternity,
Spawning so many tiny, helpless fry,
A vast blue lolling thing, a sight once to view
And smell – ere we die.

The sea, the sea, wrecker of men's lives,
And their parent too,
Through rough waters they sail on so true.

The sea, the sea, can I once conceive its form,
Its span, grave depths, creativity, moods,
Both cold and warm?

Surely all human passion is there,
With one proviso: it is never guilty of its crimes,
Much less does it care.

Sumatra Road, NW6

I enter Sumatra Road
On a hot and sunny day in June,
Searching for the dwelling
Where one of my ancestors,
My great-grandmother
On my father's side,
His mother's mother,
Once resided…long ago.

The terraced houses of this street
Are small and well kept,
Several newly painted.
The gardens are neat and orderly,
With many a lively shrub in full bloom.

If only, before I had left
And turned this way,
As if by chance,
Only recognising once the name,
I had asked my father
And taken note
(When he were still alive),
The number and address,
Or scanned the electoral roll,
For women by then, had the vote.

Some way on, the sun,
Heating my forehead in
A pleasant caress, I came across
The old lady, bespectacled,
Sitting on the steps outside,
Engaging the weather,
All dressed in grey.

I stopped to take off
My thin red pullover, now more
Than a burden to me.

"Lovely day" I said, pausing briefly.
She at first made no answer,
Being hard of hearing,
Well into her eighties
I should guess.

"Yes it is", she replied…
Suddenly, which made me jump
Between the question and answer,
Now unexpected.

"And don't you go picking a
Fight with it", she continued
In her Irish brogue,
"Or it might just get up and run away!"

I smiled, almost laughed
At the simile…
And the metaphor of her race,
Always ready for a friendly chat
And if necessary, a spat…
Though not on this warm
And beautiful day, I thought.

I answered, "No, I won't" and we parted
As we had met, happy strangers
Along Sumatra Road,
Ever glad to have coincided.

Strimmers

Why is it that the gardeners with their toys,
Their strimmers, make so much noise,
And will cut off all the heads of the wild flowers
In the verges, so becoming, a beauteous
Array, which really annoys those who adore
The countryside? They are as foolish boys.

Goodbye dandelion, buttercup and cow parsley,
Which make the meadows fit for kings, or peers,
Hello empty green sward, nothing to applaud,
And only a place for bitter regret and sullen tears,
Or ball games, with their transient cheers.

Where will the butterflies mate and hide,
Or lay their eggs on their food plants, as they fast
Ride the sunshine, or dance amidst the growing host?
And maybe one day soon become extinct, pinned out behind
Dirty glass in closeted ranks, nothing but a ghost
Of spring times glorious and now, alas, long past.

Sunspot

We have a little sunspot…
In our garden, facing west,
Where the bees visit the *Ribes* bush,
And the blackbird builds her nest.

Where the tulips, with ragged flower,
Cerise and strident red,
Adorn the crowded borders
To fill the lovely bed.

Cowslips bloom and honesty pays
In the corners by the lawn,
With vivid, bold colours
To greet the expectant dawn.

The hoverflies and bee flies
Attend the dandelion's mane,
Escapee from the gardener's eye,
Beneath the kerria's flame.

Whilst in the beech tree, tall, near by,
Still denuded of leaves,
The wood pigeon calls out repetition,
As the swift o'erhead fast weaves.

And slowly in this quiet, busy spot,
With the sun warm on the face,
All the diverse sounds of nature
Dictate the rambling pace.

Water falls, a distant flow,
The children laugh and play,
As hours and minutes coalesce
On this long bank holiday.

Thank the Lord, or whosoever,
For this vital, secret place,
Where life's cares evaporate
Amidst the soon forgotten race.

The Goat

Over elm beams the black goat peers,
Gazing through long floppy ears,
Awaiting with full ripe udder,
Milking and expected fodder.

A thin face and slitty eyes,
Of what does it surmise,
Of us who look back in surprise
Who only give to take its prize?

Milk, cheese, kid or hair,
Or what else it can spare,
But please not its skin, its hide,
For this, I guess, it'd rather wear.

Snowdrops

Snowdrops
Shed a tender tear or two,
And juggle
In the cold, bright wind,
White, the outer petals pure,
They possess no sin
To offend the innocent dawn.

But once lift a flower
Between thumb and forefinger, –
To stare with adoration
Into that little brave crown
With lime green lines
And yellow anthers,
A heart within…

Knowing that, on some warmer
February day
Than this…
At last,
The drowsy fly or bee
Must visit
To set its seed…
So that we may witness
Perennial beauty,
For one more year…

Before the Sun has charmed
The hail and snow
That fell across the land,
And below the copper beech
Where the snowdrops now hide,
To cover much of the garden.

A surprise when we awoke,
When the curtains were fully
Drawn this day,
Some while before Easter
And those showy, gilded
Bells appear.

Where the Iguassu falls

A panorama of epic stance,
A great wide step
Where waters dance
And throw away their lot
To fickle chance,
Both left and right.
The river falls determined
Straight down…to its end
In places,
Plummeting two hundred feet,
It sprawls
On the flat, jagged rocks below.

In hair-like silver strands
It dangles past the cliffs,
Showering the rugged, wavering plants –
Liverworts and grasses amongst them,
Clinging tight against the flood
For all their worth.

In seething torrents,
Streaked with plumes of algal green,
It bursts the gap, desperate in its release,
Torrents roar in mass cascades,
Slipping and tumbling in frantic escape,
To boil and spit
Near the steady, punished earth.

More frightening,
It descends the Devil's Throat
In awesome and terrible spate;
Irate and without restraint
It breaks into fuming clouds
To curse and split
The very light itself –

A rainbow, almost circular,
High above the gorge
With its maelstrom
And coursing river far, far down...

Down to where
Little orange rubber boats
Ply their trade...
For the sake of fun.
Motors whirring and brave souls,
Though never Braves,
Scream out their lungs;
Fight hard against the current
To test their nerves to destruction
Against the fury of the race.

As the river thus reformed
Flows fast ahead
To point its arrow head
Through boulders
Amidst the foaming tide...

It calms, the pace
Slackening until, with grace,
It leaves quiet and sedate, almost tamed,
Into broader, calmer plains.

Here the distant twittering swallows,
With clear white backs,
Dart and swing around
The water's face...

An exact inversion
Of the vultures floating way above
Effortlessly, in the sunlit blue...
Wings outstretched,
They soar and glide
To stare in dark, unmoved solemnity

Over the strife and struggles
In microcosm...
That some angels fear to tread
Amongst the living and perhaps the dead:
Thrown back on choppy waves,
Their fate in God's hands.

When all is said and done...
And beyond the cataract's many voices,
The jungle spreads out,
Stretching serene to the point
Of no return...

Where the sun
Breaks brilliant
In the quivering east,
Through the morning mist...
Arising with the butterflies
And the rare, awkward cries
Of many a gorgeous forest bird,
Sometimes ...and with mystery,
Discerned.

Orange Tips

It is gladdening to see the male orange tips
Scouting the rich meadow,
Stocked well with dandelions and buttercups,
All rivals to eclipse their show.

The Pine Cone

In dinosaur days it also fell
To land in unknown ground,
Long before the present craze
Was laid so neatly
Up on a hill, little in time to those
Giant feet, those footprints
Triple clawed, that
Here sped their way
Towards a dripping Sun,
Much hotter than
Its weak descendant now
Can give;
It stays, hardly abused
Where smaller rushing toes
And heels press underway
Towards a time
Whose goal is better set,
But not much wiser
In the fullness of an eye's blink,
Where creatures big and small,
Rarely think
Between savage meals...
The pine cone
Lies still, as it has mostly ever done,
Its hard, smooth, resinous hands open
As the mists run off
And the air dries to a silky skin...
Lets go the tight-stowed seeds,
Germens all
That slip into the soil
To bristle in weeks yet to come....
Whilst callous deer
Nibble their tender shoots
And reduce them to a lean and skinny pole –
As in dinosaur days –

73

When horny beaks and peg-like teeth
Crumpled those scrumptious tips
In a land beyond our ken.

The Movie

We sit in our armchairs
To watch the 'movie'
In comfort.
A soap opera of life?
A natural history film?
A re-enactment of some
Battle of long ago?

The speakers deliver us soothing
Music – Pachalbel's Canon.
Maybe guns of a lesser sort.

The cool air plays
Around our golden locks.

Our beloved remains throughout
By our side.
On we stare through clear, curved glass.

We see hills and valleys, strange panoramas
Indeed, little villages, crowded city streets.

Sometimes it rains, or snows,
Or the picture is misty and unclear.

We feel a detachment from the real world.
A sense of sublime security, contentment.
It is relatively quiet and warm.
Even the children and the dog behave,
Playing happily behind our forward gaze.

Only the speedometer
Tells the extravagant lie
That registers
One mistake…and then
Perhaps…we could die.

Ambition

Ambition is but vanity,
A kind of restless insanity
That drives men to extremes
To fulfil their boundless dreams –
An age-old scourge of humanity.

The Fortress

Why do they hide away…
Locked up like squirrels in their autumnal drey?
Is it the Vikings or Saxons they are frightened of,
Or perhaps it's the Russians, the dreaded Oblomov
That keeps them secreted, but afraid of whom;
Some particular worry, a prescience of doom?

Few birds are cuckoos, most are honest folk
That hatch from the egg, reared on the yolk;
The chances of encounter are exceedingly slim,
Yet in birds' minds, the reality is grim.

So too of they that hide behind walls,
That fear and shudder as the deceitful calls,
And fearing of robbery, pillage…and worse,
Lend themselves slaves…to this ancient curse.

No fortress is foolproof, safe from attack,
Especially when unguarded, away at the back.
The impression of security is what cheers men's minds,
Safe behind curtains, safe behind blinds.

But where is that castle whose walls are so strong
That has resisted intruders, down ages so long?
No my friends, from this it is patently clear,
That common-sense now…is the poor dupe of fear.

The Greek Ferry [†]

The ship on which the Muse might sail,
Left the port to no avail,
Tossed by waves in a savage sea,
Never to claim its bright destiny.

Racing hard to make for land,
Guided by a dead man's hand,
Cruel rocks loom high from raging spray,
The sirens' songs now loud convey.

Like an arrow hell-bent on its course,
Mean banshees blow with all their force,
Until the rending of iron and steel —
A deafening fracture, a tortured squeal.

In minutes the vessel violent turns,
Absent from the bridge, the Captain learns
His ship is slipping fast to sink,
Into salt waters as black as ink.

Whilst in those waters, babes make haste,
Their scrambling parents doomed to waste,
When suddenly, in that darkest night,
Are seen heavenly lumens, a distant light.

Whirring motors, high above,
A rescue dangled from a metallic dove,
Some souls are plucked from the glaring eye,
Whilst their comrades soon must die.

In grim surrounds, lashing wet,
The rescuer's heart, their only debt,
And in the morning, a sultry Sun,
The seas are cleared and onward run.

The tides between the islands spread;
Now sad tinged with cherry red...
To mark the grave and tranquil scene;
To taunt what seems to have never been.

† The MS *Express Samina*, wrecked off the island of
  Paros in the Aegean on the night of Tuesday
  26th September, 2000.

Green Man

How strange.
As I stare into the entangled Clematis mass
That adorns the south-facing wall,
Its leaves much retarded
In this most prolonged
And cool of Aprils,
I see a face, old and venerable,
Return my stare.

Bearded and moustachioed,
With bushy eyebrows;
He appears wise beyond even his years.

Is it the face of Christ, as perhaps
It should be this Easter weekend,
Reminding us of his pain
And sacrifice…and our fortune?

Or merely the Green Man,
Token inhabitant of the ancient, gnarled
Oak, beech and ash woodlands
Of England; the pagan king?

I break my stare…and then
Rejoin; he is still there.

I break again…and return.
Then he is gone…
And I can only marvel at such tricks
Of the eye and mind.

Strange glimpses of the sighted blind.
And hopefully, not a warning…
To beware.

After the Thunderstorm

It is one thirty five in the morning.
We lie in bed, listening to the storm unfold
Over our heads, our roof. Roll after roll
Of artillery fire, the lightening and thunder
Breaks to make us start and fear
For the safety of the house...
And our lives.

The yellow curtains light up momentarily...
Only to subside once again into darkness.

We count the seconds between
The flashes and the crash of thunder...

Then it breaks
A incredible blast, such
That the heavens shake.

It is now only some two miles away.

The storm continues for at least
An hour. Heavy rains begin, torrential, unrelenting
In their voracity (although the wind remains calm).

We wonder how the river is,
And the people in the new houses
In the valley, built on the flood plain.
Will the water come up over the bridge
As it has nearly done many times
This wet autumn, winter and spring?
Or will it also subside away,
The houses again courting disaster, only to be saved?

I get up to look through the window...
I am impressed at what I see.

Then however, the flashes weaken, the intervals
Between light and sound increase…as the storm
Slowly moves off, animate, growling like some great
Beast departing back to its lair.

In the morning, the robins appear again,
Husband and wife, soaked and bedraggled…
But still alive. The cock bird feeds his hen
With a morsel plucked from the hebe bush nearby.
Perhaps a juicy caterpillar –
I did not see exactly what his gift was…
Other than it was so.

They then continue to inspect
The old, green ceramic teapot in the hedge
(Placed there some years before in anticipation
Of their acceptance, but never used until now)…
And carefully place beech leaves in it to build their nest.
Sometimes, soon after, they pull them
All out…as if dissatisfied.
This, to our amusement, goes on all morning.
On one occasion they abandon their work,
Only to return the next day to restart the process.

By now, the storm is a faint memory, both to them
And to us…

Only the thick carpet of pink petals under the
Ornamental cherry reveals the true ferocity
Of events…and the river's
Spate, roaring purposefully between
The pillars of the bridge.

Whilst the robins sing, the sun comes out
As we finish our coffee and discuss the storm.
I say that "I cannot remember such a storm
Since I was a child."

But probably I am wrong. Time both tempers
The storm and one's memory of it.
Nevertheless, last night was incredible.

The Oak Tree [†]

At the swinging sign
Of the old 'Oak Tree',
On which the English plant itself
Is depicted quite mightily,
There an irony exists,
Which strangely persists
Down the ages,
Nearly as long
As I can remember.

The landlord smiles benevolently
And pulls his beer,
His whole deportment friendly
And of good cheer
So no one has the heart
To tell him,
Decidedly not that durable
Hard-grained variety...

That the great tree standing
Nearby in the grounds,
Whose autumn foliage
Is now turning a rusty brown,
Is in truth a Turkey...
Not an English oak!

If only he too had seen
Those long, dark green,
Heavily serrated leaves...
Then it would have
Been sooner known,
That he...and the tree,
Were originally from...
Different nations...

Never mind.
Together they make
A fine team,
The best pub, landlord, beer...
And tree...in town.

† Harpenden, Hertfordshire.

Youth

Clutch the future with those untarnished hands,
Embrace you bright souls of the young.
Enjoy the music your parents never sung,
Race along without a care –
For the hell of it, or for the dare.
Dance the night away until you drop,
Until your ringing ears almost pop.
Wear strange fashions that ever shock,
Pierce your flesh with rings…
And lock away all that is old and tired.
With new zest and when inspired,
Endorse weird ideas, skip and jump,
Bang the drum and shout and thump.
Climb mountains when the snow is down…
When wise heads gasp and frown.
Overtake and 'never say die';
Challenge old dogmas, disprove the lie.
Stare into Beauty's glass, that reflecting pool;
Play the hero, act the fool.
Only when with trembling hand,
You actually survive and sometimes win,
Do not accept that awful sin –
Middle age and worse to come.
Life's great now, so enjoy the fun!

The Frog

How does the frog view its tadpole stage
Seen from the perspective of its golden age
As it stares into the mirror of its 'geburtstag' pond
As the sun's rays penetrate the fern's green frond?

To dapple and shade the translucent spawn
Each an eye, its dark pupil staring back defiantly,
Sometimes quivering as the little soul within
Wriggles to makes its presence felt.

Soon this mass of jelly will hatch and the hatchlings
Emerge to feed rapaciously on algae, insect larvae…
And their siblings in the mud below, whilst they too
Come to quiver at the water's edge, collective,
Prepared, expectant.

They grow fast. One day, tiny limbs sprout
From their round, black bodies. Their eyes bulge in
Disbelief, as politician's do.

As the legs grow, the tadpoles' urge to leave the water rises.

They emerge, primitive tailed frogs,
'Scarce half made up', hybrids, an echo
From an age even before reptiles ruled the Earth.
Arrested, somehow in time, yet evolved.

Does an adult frog perceive all this in its mind, or just the
Strangeness of its young, happy and skipping
On the wet lawn, as the sun rises in the early dawn?

As its jaw gapes wide, so wide…to stifle a late yawn…
Or perchance, prepare to devour…one of its very own.

One God or Two?

Are there indeed two gods?
One male and one female.
One black and one white.
One young, the other old.
One right, one wrong.
One kind, the other cruel.
One sexual, one asexual.
One straight, one gay.
One big, one small.
One short, the other tall.
Light and dark; good and bad;
Positive and negative; just and unjust;
Short-sighted and far-sighted.
Imaginative and intelligent,
Dumb and dull.

The god of the Old Testament
Is war-like, wrathful, vengeful,
Bold, intolerant; that of the New,
Pacifist, benign, shy, reticent,
Tolerant, a lover of all
Mankind, not just one tribe
Or creed, as he turns
The other cheek.

Nature too can be kind or cruel,
And perhaps there lies the truth…
That there are perceived states
But in reality…and in the wider world
And struggle, only survival is the ultimate god…
Of the body and the genes…
And that the soul must look
For another house to inhabit…
Beyond the secular mortal self.
Beyond the stars themselves.

To the statistician, there is the 'normal distribution'
With its population mean and variance,
Stretching from minus infinity to plus infinity.
If the variants are selected, compete and survive
And indeed thrive, they tend to evolve.

Evolution is a god, but not of the conventional mould.
Unlike most others, it has lasted the arduous,
Unflagging test of geological time…

Beyond life, the earth, stars, material universe…
Is God.

The Winner

All seemed to be going well,
The mountain nearly climbed,
The summit glistening yards above,
The task nearly sealed and signed.

But then the leader said…'Have a rest',
So he sat and admired the view,
And in a trice a blizzard came,
And blew, and blew and blew.

And quickly he lost his way,
And sat down upon a boulder,
Where he remained for quite a while,
Only to become much colder.

The blizzard calmed within a day,
The sunshine broke right through,
Although alas, the climber stayed,
Still unsure what he must do.

He could go up, he could go down,
Yet finishing is much the finer,
He must push on and scale the heights
And become a much-praised winner!

For to fail, to fall, to go back down
Is a thing most hard to swallow,
Although only the Fates can surely know
Whether life will be rich or fallow.

Time, the Final Frontier

Four months on
And we have surpassed our goal,
Travelled further than ever
We may have dared hope…
All these years ago
When beetles first swarmed
Over still rolling stones…
And eagles soared overhead,
Undisturbed and much adored.

A lost world,
Now history in the minds
Of men…and children alike…
Especially the latter…
Who cannot begin to conceive
Of the turning of a century,
Much less an epoch's fall.

The last century now lies
Crumpled, a dinosaur, its bones
Exposed beyond its taut, grey skin,
To reveal the vagaries
Of the wind, and the critic's eye.

There is much to criticise –
Cruelty, intolerance, horror,
Injustice – and all the dark
Forces of Man's make-up…
Behind the mask.

But there was also joy too.

That we may not share,
Save for what is recorded…
And what makes us up…
And straddles our genes.

We are now as far from that era
As if it were a million years past, –
Ten millions or more.

Yes, we have artefacts,
Even memories of the chapter's turn…
Though never can those ever-fading
Pages be re-turned, save in our minds
And perhaps those of our beasts, –
For example, the sentient cat.

Time has moved on.

It alone *is* the final frontier.

We can move in space,
But unless we traverse time,
That strangest of dimensions,
We are just fodder
For historians and the worm's palate…
And doomed ever to speculate
On its nature.

The Man in the Jacket, Quite Yellow

The man in the jacket,
Quite yellow,
Walks up the steep hill
Each day, despite his injuries;
The fall that made him ill.
A friendly soul, he stops for a chat
To pass away an hour,
And to show his wound too –
A ghastly sight –
That makes strong men cower –
And wonder how such courage
Can persist, at that...
Indeed, how flesh can resist
This onslaught to the bone
That makes the observer, but never the man,
Sigh or groan.
That brave young fellow
In the coat so pure,
A coat of the brightest yellow.

Where have you been?
(In homage to a nursery rhyme)

Where have you been my treasured one?
Is it to find some peace
From me, or to set out for lands anew,
To search for the golden fleece?

Birds of Passage

No, we're just birds of passage,
Crossing the great, wide 'Pond',
Skimming high over the shimmering waves,
As we head fast, on and on...

Towards landfall, on we go,
Towards the orange setting sun,
Still brilliant in the western sky,
As the day is not yet done.

To reach the misty seaboard,
To bathe in warm tropic seas,
To feel the warmth on our bodies,
To enjoy a life of ease.

But here also we have other roles,
That we must still assume,
To walk side by side in harmony
To the sound of a different tune.

To tie the knot and pledge our troth
That we are as but one,
To live and learn and appreciate,
A love that we so yearn.

To stroll along that shoreline
At the fall of the city light,
As stars amongst the stars we are
And wow, do we shine bright!

The Smew

Today I saw a smew…
I had a good view
Of it, down by the flooded Saale river;
A handsome bird it was too, a male
Bright black, grey and white, it's perfectly true.
But now, what shall I do?

Should I add its name to some old book
Hoping that, one day, the world would be
Suitably shook …
Or rather, add it to the world-wide-web,
So that it can instantly swim towards other such
Birds…and birders,
And perhaps, just perhaps,
One sighting will eventually become two.

Lavender

I can smell lavender
Adrift in the air;
It permeates the bedroom...
And your gorgeous hair.

To My Love

To my love with all my love
On this joyous, happy day,
When all is calm perfection
Now the clouds have rolled away…

And the sun shines from a sapphire sky
As it roams both warm and bright
To catch the celandine's open eye
And fill it with radiant light.

At the lime tree's massive roots,
They swarm like brilliant stars,
Yellow drops of purest gold
That caress and kiss the hours…

And make me look forward…and realise
The measure of life's full worth,
In hope for the future
Another twenty years on earth…

To be with my fair beloved
And sail the seven seas,
Or walk the enchanted forests
And wander as we please…

But nowhere in this awakening land
Or another more distant call
Can we ever reclaim that present debt,
Those small blooms say it all.

Then I returned slowly homeward,
Down Coach Lane, a sunlit path,
And watched two magpies take to wing
And heard the Yaffles laugh.

Thus somewhere out there, I knew by heart,
Our love would long remain,
The world revolve, the seasons pass,
From flowers and birds, t'was plain.

Clouded Yellow [†]

The clouded yellow flies ever fast,
No sooner noticed than almost past,
On its quest for lucerne and clover
From the groves of Greece to the cliffs at Dover.

In England, a species rarely seen
Across the landscape varied green,
First spanning the seas of restless blue,
A yellow beacon it is most true.

Traversing the distant reaches of the earth,
Flying strongly for all its worth,
A spirit of hot summer days,
It soon dies out and never stays...

The course of our approaching winter
When frosts crack and sometimes splinter
The very rocks of this our land,
Preferring southern climes and warm, dry sand...

Where its eggs are laid and larvae feed
Upon those plants of leguminous breed,
A sight to gladden the English heart,
Bright flame, stay long and ne'er depart.

If only in our fleeting mind
Before one day comes back your kind
To dance across flower-rich meadows,
Though where and when...one never knows,

† *Colias croceus* Geoffroy

August Moon

I am sorry that you are too busy
To study the Moon…as once you did with me,
To swoon and pant under its giddy, luminous
Disc in June, or its more mysterious presence
In July, and even more so in August,
When it appears cream yellow against a gunmetal
Sky…at nine, obscured by ribbons of thin cloud,
Almost benign.

We resign ourselves to its rule,
Hoping that what we take for granted now
May one day prove true.
That Selene will stay faithful
To those who worship her, or at least
Acknowledge her eternal, celestial station.

Not a sound can be heard right now
As I prepare to leave, and take one last look
Skyward toward the south-east,
Where love may yet reside,
As it surely does here in this small enclave,
Near the lake.

So please come and join me
To view the Moon…
And once more re-unite our souls with tranquillity…
And a small flicker of romance.

City of Flitwick

Oh City of Flitwick
Is your fate surely known?
What of development? –
My how you've grown!
No longer a village, hardly a town,
Will your character be cherished,
Or rude away thrown?
And what of your admirers
Who care how you stay?
Will their views be respected,
Or tossed, too, away?
Your church and green spaces,
Pubs, quaint and old,
Will they be bulldozed,
The land swiftly sold?
Will concrete and chaos
Rule full supreme,
With offices and factories?
My, how they gleam!
And what of the people
Whose place this still is,
Will they soon awaken,
Or continue to zizz?
For things are afoot now,
Menacing they loom
To make Flitwick bigger…
Quite vast I assume.

So goodbye to peace,
Birds, hedgerows and all…
And prepare for the Contractors…
And builders…to call.

2001

Here it is, two thousand and one,
Despite the strange new date,
The Sun still shines on
As it has always done,
And the bumblebees
Inspect the geranium flowers,
Bright purple-blue,
As they have always done,
To my recollection,
And will, I hope,
Always do,

Fifty Years on
(Requiem for the 1914-18 war)

Under the warm sun of time's remorse
We stroll unconscious as the blind man's day,
Through fields of morning and silent pause,
Through painful memories; what senseless cause.

Now with war, fear and hate remote,
Suppressed within the hearts of Englishmen,
The toll of strife's harvest is taken note;
In Freedom's cause all were smote.

Once more the poppies of the mind quick spread
Across the scarred and bloody dales,
They conceal and hide what generals said,
But not the bleached bones of England's dead.

The Poet's Lot

Next to unchanging love,
Loyalty and youth
It really is above
Exception
For one who writes verse
To win a publisher's
Few terse
Words of praise,
Or even raise
The slightest interest
In what he feels, thinks and says,
In poetry (he hopes) his literary best.

And yet the works
Of the 'Establishment' continue on,
They who deserve, perhaps, a little rest,
Thus to allow
An eager Public
To learn a new poet's
Flowing rhymes...

And maybe also,
Let him derive
From his writer's cramp,
Some Royalties,
A meagre living such to earn.

Oh indeed these are unhappy times
For they who live
In cold, damp surrounds,
Putting Art before wealth (and heat)
Purely on aesthetic grounds.

Home

Home is where your heart is,
Wherever you may be,
In far-flung lands across the waves,
In lands of uncertainty.

It doesn't matter about the climate,
The food, or language too,
Whether you can speak it fluently,
Of just a few words, most few.

Nor does it matter about religion,
Belief in the one true god,
Or clothing, or the exchange rate,
Or living on one's tod.

It only matters that you have faith,
A belief in truth and yourself,
And good works and honesty,
And a smattering of good health.

And of course, in one's love ones,
The joy of your lonely heart,
So that they are always with you,
When you needs must depart.

And board a plane and fly away
To a small island on a map,
Where palm trees grow and mangos fall
Right into your very lap.

Only then can your really discern
The wisdom of the ways,
That geography is of little worth,
What matters is what fills your heart.

Foreign Dogs

Are Rottweilers vile rotters,
Dachshunds just hot dogs,
Pekingese cool pooches...
And Poodles mere frogs?

Spitze social climbers,
Pyreneans aiming high,
Chows some kind of chop suey,
And their puppies mere stir fry?

Afghans hairy bitches,
Spaniels daft as a brush,
Boston terriers very butch,
And dingoes straight from the bush?

Surely Boxers like shorts,
Highland terriers good malt,
Irish wolfhounds large snorts...
Whilst only English bulldogs...

...the lot assault.

Kookaburra's Laugh

From way up on Goodearth's glistening heights
We look across Brisbane's brash new sights.
We also hear from our high-perched cell,
All the city's sounds, clear as a bell.

Traffic – trams, buses, cars, horns,
Much building noise too:
All greet this morning in their variety true.

But the native birds
Refuse to be out done:
Grey butcher birds, kookaburras, rosellas, crows;
A plethora of species, God only knows;
Cry out with raucous or haunting melodic airs;
Look down from eucalypts
And wattles with hypnotic stairs.

Determined that they will hang on and yet still rule,
Be the weather fearsome hot or as now, rainy cool…

After all, they were here first,
Long before Europeans and Progress
On this scene burst.

They cry out that they are here to stay,
And jibe aloud that Man may soon…
Well… like the flowers, just fade away.

A Day Spent at Tenby
11th September, 2006

We walked the south beach at Tenby
Along near endless golden sand,
With thoughts of Delius and Fenby[†],
Or love held hand in hand.

The sea a glistening prospect,
Oyster catchers piped their call,
Whilst grey clouds silent scudded,
And young dogs played the fool.

Thence back to the pastel town itself,
Perched high on massive rocks,
Through dark curtain walls,
To browse bric-a-brac and rare, old books.

In the pub we ate our sandwiches,
Made from good Welsh beef,
Still with thoughts most musical,
And a new found belief.

That the future is surely rosy,
That failure is not allowed,
That self-doubts are not de rigeur,
And of achievements, we should be proud.

Thus we closed the day most happy,
As content as two can be,
Down by the coast of Tenby,
With the beach…and you…and me.

[†] In remembrance of the orchestral work *A Song of Summer* (1929-32) composed by Frederick Delius (1862-1934) with assistance from Eric Fenby, OBE (1906-97).

The Moth

Hello moth, what are you up to?
Flying across the patio window pane with such design,
Such urgency?

Are you seeking the light too?
A religious light, now much dimmed
In this oh so secular world.

Or just seeking that 'forbidden fruit', nectar, as heavy with
Promise as a fermented pear.

I do not ask you so precisely.
It would be rude, and maybe unwise.

But I wish you well on your trip
Back into the night…

You brown, fluttering, mysterious dude,
He of the red, fluorescent, blood-shot eyes.

The Last Day of 2005

It is the last day of two thousand and five…

A time to reflect…and strive;
To grapple with and unravel
All those issues and complexities
That confront us in our daily lives;
To contemplate the unknowable and unforeseen,
The might be and what has never been;
The shining ball striking the pin
In the pinball machine…

And also to stop awhile,
To view what we have now,
Regardless of fate and her fickle finger –
Friendship, love, awareness, understanding
And contentment…

Although 'tis true, the great rolling world
Is never still, never at rest…
And rolls on regardless
Of our plans, our hopes,
Fears, designs and zest…

It was, after all, here long before
We were a twinkle in the stars,
Sown wildly in our parent's eyes…

And will be long after we
Have found them again in the enormity
Of what we call Space,
A huge, desolate place for sure…
Yet it is all we have…

Beyond the confines of our gorgeous
Blue, teeming planet,
Home of a myriad fascinating species.

Travels Abroad

If it's not the jiggers trying to bite your toes,
It's the cercaria going up your nose,
Or the sharks trying to bite your bum
Or the mosquitoes your little thumb!

On Kings, Cola and Zola [†]
(At the Königsplatz, Augsburg, Germany)

Let us sit upon that wall and drink our old king Cola
And laugh and joke and play the fool and recite the words of Zola.

[†] Emile Zola (1840-1902), French novelist.

Beauty

He who loves her must grasp the hour,
The minute, the second, pluck the flower,
That divine bloom which turns men's heads,
And distracts their minds...awake...or asleep
Their restless beds.

Revenge on the Ash Tree

Poor tree, what had it done except wave its arms
And look beautiful in the sun.

Here songbirds sang in its lofty boughs,
Linnet, chaffinch, thrush, singing long and hard,
All the 'hows' and 'whys'
Of their complex lives, the many secrets known to them
That Time and evolution had bequeathed.
A hymn to the beauty of divine form and kind,
Too abstract for the distracted mind
That dwells on throughout the blustery days
Of March, when snows blow rough
Through the sacred, naked crown,
And obscure the early spring rays
Of hope.

Here also the chequered woodpecker drummed
Out his message smart;
The squirrels played like strong, grey cats high up,
To soon depart in leaps and bounds,
From branch to branch, skipping great leaps
Of faith as is their stance
In life.

Alas the tree had offended. It dropped leaves and twigs...
To the very earth and ground from which it came...
And so had to die.

Now only a few branches are left to nod and cry
Out their lament for the wind...
Such is their legacy – a mutilated relic by and by...
Of former glory and a sad end indeed
To a once beauteous story.

Fie I say unto thee…
Who had complicity and conspiracy in its wounds;
As with Christ and the Cross; they who missed its glad tidings,
And were deaf to its mute, yet happy sounds.

Nb. The Ash tree was a sacred tree in ancient British culture,
including in Ireland: 'Assemblies were held under these trees and
it was sacrilegious to damage them in any way'. (Morton, A. 1986.
The Trees of Shropshire: Myth, Fact and Legend. Airlife Publishing Ltd.,
Shrewsbury, England, pp.114)

Awakening

Must I get up and face the world
out of this half light of awakening dawn,
out from these warm sheets
where my beloved lies uncurled?

Must I get up and face the world
and launch a thousand ships
that cruise a glistening sea
with golden sails unfurled?

Must I get up and face the world
and send an army across the blistering plains
to besiege the dewy heights of Kabul
where seemingly wrath is often hurled?

Or can I lie here a little longer in bed
and frame some poetic thoughts…
that some think exist below this lurking skull
but seem today elusive, evading my vapid head?

Must I get up and face the world?
I fear I must…and rise up…yes, and
in the spirit of adventure too…

Since at any rate, my love, my muse,
is still fast asleep, as her soft, kissable, flickering
eyelids prove…whilst lovely dreams continue
to swarm… as once in her deepest mind,
they swirled.

Upon visiting Rothamsted Manor Gardens
12th September, 2003

Often, for a moment...
as if lost amidst a dallying rhyme,
I sit in the Manor gardens
on that stone seat,
carved and ancient,
covered as it is in the grime
of ages and yellow lichens few...

To gaze due south across the lawn;
across clipped yew hedges,
the small pool with its beautiful naked statue,
a girl, and rose bushes fair...

To the great house with its Dutch gables,
Tudor chimneys and walls of mellow-coloured brick,
so warm when the autumn sun plays upon its face...

And the virginia creeper
turning vermilion, which threatens to
mask the leaden windows and their cool,
dark, mysterious interiors beneath...
where ambition, frustration, love, indeed life itself
have been enacted,
or sometimes hatched in the quiet solitude.

And on I stare into that midday hour...
beyond the giant lime trees, brightest green –
the fallen apples that adorn the sward –
towards the Redbourn Road,
towards St. Albans itself...

As St. Peter's church bells –
too far to be heard from here –

toll out their peals of joy and sadness,
especially on a Saturday morning,
telling the world that a couple have wed,
that a child is baptised, or a citizen dead.

In that time, I remember too…
a brief remembrance of summers
most glorious days, when shrill swifts
slice the air in dashing haste…

Before I drift to the herbaceous border,
strewn with drying flowers in immaculate order,
to watch whilst yarrow, ice plants and asters mauve
play host to a tribe of butterflies,
small coppers all, that dance a little minuet,
a lovely ball on a flower's most brilliant head,
and follow and flirt with me
on my way out from paradise…

Out past the red oak with its dying leaves,
large and concealed,
behind a wood of laurels, never seemingly at rest,
where a good friend lies scattered,
his ashes at its roots…

Poor young Phil', brave soul,
too good for this world (and too ill)…
and perhaps for the world beyond.
Now just a memory…
and even whilst he lived, he was somehow
but a fleeting presence in the flickering panoply
of time.

Today the air seems hotter than before,
the sun harsher and the force of its rays,
demanding of me in its praise…

Then the Manor bell strikes two, a haunting call,
clear yet muted as if untrue.
I leave this place, vowing to return.
Certainly tomorrow, if the sun is warm…
and the collared doves continue
to coo from on high
in the tallest branches of the purple beech,
witness of the centuries flow…

And if butterflies still swarm
and dance on gorgeous blooms…
so that my love of this spot continues – as ever –
to grow.

† Philip Manning (1947-78), photographer at Rothamsted
Research, Harpenden, Herts., U.K., from 1970-73.

What are you thinking my love?

On the train journey heading south,
facing you in the opposite seat,
I study your beautiful features,
yet you seem almost a stranger
on this bright August day in the heat.
What are you thinking my love?

We seem to traverse a strange land indeed,
you and I, half a world away…or so it seems,
above the dark, swirling waters
of the Thames …
and the rust-red, rickety rails
that sometimes threaten
to cast us all down…and there to drown…

We jolt from side to side
and view agog the Victorian scene…
beyond the tenements, graffiti
and broken skyline of old London…
not quite one.

A vision of decay relieved only
by the river itself; St. Paul's dome,
Tower Bridge, Canary Wharf Tower,
The London Eye (ever wary),
and the daring new glass and steel
of the erotic 'Gherkin' and 'Glass egg',
both interesting as they are crazily unique.

Sometimes your expression seems lost,
fraught, or cross; sometimes happy and serene…
as fleeting clouds that seek to block the mighty Sun…
but eventually give way…
to let the warming, benevolent rays

through, – hence please both the land
and 'all [the] people that on earth do dwell.'

I trust that I am not such an imposing cloud...
because my love, what I feel for you is fair,
and lovely, and true it must be said...
as well as ever proud.

Sorry not for us

'Sorry not for us' she said,
As a wry smile passed briefly
Across her pursed, thin lips;
'Sorry not for us' she said
As she signed the letter
To reject…and close the case;
'Sorry not for us' she said
As she picked up the manuscript
As if by the ears,
To reject it, hurriedly,
To the basket –
Its final resting place?

Or perhaps like that scene
When with one outstretched arm…
A whiffy rat, somewhat dead,
Is deposited in the bin!

But have no fear; the manuscript cannot die,
For it has no breath as such,
And though some would wish it so,
Now is not the time
To lay that flaccid wreath.

The Flame of Fame
(Fire and Water)

The flame of fame
Is ever fickle.
To begin with, a simple trickle,
Then ultimately a flood,
A torrent, a tsunami,
Gushing through channels,
Cutting broad valleys...
Before it subsides,
To become, one fine day,
A faint, indistinguishable trickle
Once more.

Mauve Gladioli

Like Marilyn Monroe,
The mauve gladioli,
Yesterday so fine,
Have collapsed
Under the burden...
Of their own beauty.

Phyllis

We found her sitting there
On a hillside, under a tree,
Watching the whole universe
Of flowers unfold.

Who's to blame

The culture of blame
Is the name of the game.
We blame everyone save ourselves,
When colliding with jutting shelves,
Or falling from a bike too big,
Or jabbing our eye with an invisible twig,
Or falling off a slippery log,
Or diving headfirst into the bog.

We like to blame our friends or kind
About the contrary blowing wind,
But surely,
Only we ourselves can claim
To lay hands on that prize…guiltless blame,
And when the fault is truly ours
We should resist with all our powers
And accept our lot with love and grace,
And bless this world, our unique place.

By the same author

The Eternal Quest (1988), Merlin Books Ltd., U.K.
(under the pseudonym Hugh Llewelyn);
Re-published 2003 by Brambleby Books as
The Eternal Quest: A celebration of nature in poetry
by Hugh David Loxdale
ISBN 9780954334710

Blue Skies in Tuscany (2000), Minerva Press Ltd., U.K.
Re-published 2003 by Brambleby Books
ISBN 9780954334727

Fascinating Felines (2002),
ISBN 9780954334703

Bird Words: Poetic images of wild birds (2003),
ISBN 9780954334734

The Jena Poems (2010)
ISBN 9780955392894

Love and the Sea (2010)
ISBN 9780955392887

Nevisian Days: Poetry from a Caribbean Isle (2011)
ISBN 9781908241009